The 'ten rules' concept sets out to be gently provocative. Sadly, the 'rules' in this booklet are reflective of many of the practices we have come across that cause so many problems for people with learning disabilities who are on the autism spectrum, and those who care for and support them, making it very difficult for them to access the quality of healthcare the rest of us take for granted.

We hope it will be a useful starting point for discussion and a catalyst for action.

'Three things in human life are important. The first is to be kind. The second is to be kind. The third is to be kind.'

Henry James

T0168002

3

About the authors

Viki Ainsworth is a journalist, copywriter and director of a media training and TV talent agency. She is also an expert by lived experience and is on parental advisory panels for Great Ormond Street Hospital and NHS England. Viki has a BSc (Econ) in International Relations, a Postgraduate Diploma in Journalism and a Postgraduate Diploma in Philosophy, and she is also an Applied Behavioural Analysis therapist.

Jim Blair is currently a Consultant Nurse Intellectual (Learning) Disabilities at Great Ormond Street Hospital, Associate Professor Intellectual (Learning) Disabilities at Kingston University and St Georges' University of London as well as Clinical Advisor Learning Disabilities NHS England. He is also the Health Advisor at the British Institute of Learning Disabilities and the Learning Disability Advisor to the Sates of Jersey and Guernsey. From 2011-2013, Jim was Vice Chairman of Special Olympics Great Britain. Jim is an Expert Advisor to the Parliamentary Health Service Ombudsman, an advisor for the Down Syndrome Medical Interest Group and is on the editorial board of www.intellectualdisability.info. Jim is also a Specialist Clinical Advisor to the Care Quality Commission.

A note on terminology

In this book we have decided to use the terms 'autistic people', and 'people on the autism spectrum' to respect the preferences of the autistic community. We have also avoided the use of the term 'patients' where possible, to suggest that, when working with autistic people, people with learning disabilities and their families, medical professionals especially need to work mutually and respect the expertise of those they work with, rather than expecting recipients of their support to be 'patient' and passive in the relationship.

Introduction

It remains a shocking fact that children and adults with learning disabilities and those on the autism spectrum continue to experience difficulty in accessing the kind of health care that is available to the rest of the population, and it is shocking how this impacts upon health outcomes. For example, a female with learning disabilities will die on average 17 years younger than an equivalent neurologically typical female, while for males with learning disabilities it is 13 years younger (Heslop *et al*, 2013). There have been all too many enquiries into unexplained deaths and failures to provide even adequate health care in hospitals and other settings. An inability to engage with the individual and their carers, and to recognise the person's healthcare needs separate from their disability, ensures that they are denied health care and treatment that others take for granted.

This book is based on the premise that positive change in healthcare practice will come from understanding a person through the medium of a relationship, and by taking account of the diverse nature of learning disabilities and autism and how the individual is likely to see and interpret the world. Intended to be provocative and challenging of our existing practice as professionals and support staff, the 'ten rules' will help staff to offer assessment, treatment and support that is based on a deeper understanding and acceptance of that person throughout their healthcare journey.

Each 'rule' speaks powerfully with the 'voice' of the individual on the receiving end of healthcare practice. Together, the ten rules provide a useful starting point for discussion and a catalyst for action. Each is followed by suggestions for positive practices. The booklet also contains additional background information on good practice, together with references and sources of further information.

The booklet has been written for anyone involved in providing health care checks, assessment, treatment or support to people with learning disabilities and on the autism spectrum, together with allied professionals, carers and students in relevant disciplines. It can be used for a wide range of purposes, including staff induction, learning disability and autism awareness training, individual professional development and reflection, and team discussions about the quality of practice and services provided.

The content has been put together by Viki Ainsworth, Expert by Lived Parental Experience, and Jim Blair, Consultant Nurse in Learning Disabilities and Associate Professor.

The 'Ten Rules' series was conceived by Richard Mills (research director, Research Autism and Hon. Research Fellow, University of Bath, visiting professor, Taisho University, Tokyo; Bond University, Australia) and Dr Damian Milton (lecturer in intellectual and developmental disabilities, Tizard Centre, University of Kent), who also edited this volume. Other titles in the series can be found on www.pavpub.com

Rule 1

Assume that you know everything and we know nothing

☢ That way you can avoid tapping into the wealth of expertise that is in the room with you.

☢ Because the healthcare system is obviously there for your benefit not ours.

☢ You've done your training and have nothing left to learn.

Positive practises

☺ You may be the healthcare expert, but don't dismiss parents, carers and support workers – they are experts at knowing what works for the individual.

☺ Ask for help! Ask colleagues, ask the parents, ask support staff and carers, ask the individual you are working with.

☺ Don't be afraid to get it wrong, just make sure you're open to learning from your mistakes.

☺ Be open to finding alternative methods of dispensing your expertise.

☺ Ask for support from learning disability nurses.

☺ It is essential to build a partnership with the individual and their carers and families to make sure you learn everything you can.

☺ The health system should be accessible and inclusive – your attitude will have a lot of influence on whether that is actually the case in practice.

Rule 2

Don't worry about how you communicate with me

☢ That way I can get really, really anxious about any interactions with you.

☢ All those other methods of communication that exist aren't useful or necessary.

☢ We don't want you to spend time and energy figuring out how to treat any people who don't fit the norm.

Positive practises

- 😊 So much of communication is non-verbal – body language, tone of voice, speed of delivery – all are cues that will elicit responses.

- 😊 Some people with learning disabilities on the autism spectrum will prefer verbal communication and are less able to pick up other cues.

- 😊 Again, ask for help – it will empower you and the individuals you are working with.

- 😊 If you are uncomfortable, angry or frustrated with the person you are seeing, you *will* communicate this to them. Being familiar with them and their preferred means of communication will put the person you are seeing at ease.

- 😊 Talk to the family, support staff and, where possible, the individual, about the best method of communication – photos, signs, symbols, accessible publications such as the Books Beyond Words series, and pictures.

- 😊 Take time, slow down, use fewer words, and check the person has understood, or where capacity is limited, that carers have understood, always remembering to adhere to the Mental Capacity Act (2005).

Don't make allowances for my disabilities or for me being autistic

☢ Don't adapt how you do things.

☢ Trying to make me fit into your boxes works really well.

☢ Go ahead and make assumptions, we're all the same after all.

Positive practises

🙂 You have a legal duty to ensure adjustments are made to enable individuals to access and receive the care and treatment they require. This is in accordance with the Equality Act (2010).

🙂 Accept that these appointments need a different approach – the more you can adapt and discover what works best, the more natural it will become for you.

🙂 When in doubt, TEACH:

- **T**ime – take time to work with the person.

- **E**nvironment – alter the environment to meet the person's needs, for example by providing quieter areas, reducing lighting and minimising waiting times.

- **A**ttitude – look for ways to make the encounter a positive one.

- **C**ommunication – see Rule 2!

- **H**elp – consider what help the person and their family, carers and support workers may need and how can you meet these needs.

Rule 4

Get really impatient and rush me through the appointment so you can get rid of me

☢ That way I won't have time to process any information you give me.

☢ Nor will I have time to figure out what's going on.

Positive practises

😊 For people with learning disabilities and those on the autism spectrum, even getting to the appointment can be an epic task – they may need time to adjust when they get to you.

😊 Try to tap into how the person communicates and interacts. Don't treat them like they're on a production line – the appointment is for their well-being not your convenience.

😊 Take a breath and park your impatience, schedule extra time where you can and see the whole person in front of you.

😊 A 'flagging' system within the hospital or GP surgery for identifying individuals with additional needs can help manage everyone's expectations.

Rule 5

Look past us and only talk to our families, carers or support workers

☢ It makes us feel good to be ignored.

☢ Being made to feel less than human like this does wonders for our self-worth.

Positive practises

🙂 It's a lonely and anxious experience being in a hospital or GP surgery for most people with learning disabilities and those on the autism spectrum. Don't increase their isolation by talking over or ignoring them – include them in conversations and aim to make a connection with them.

🙂 Remember that they are the person who knows themselves best.

🙂 Make reasonable adjustments to make sure the person is as comfortable as possible.

🙂 Find out if the hospital has a learning disability nurse. If not, ask to have support from a community learning disability nurse via your local community learning disability team.

Rule 6

Assume that anything I do that you find difficult is part of my disability and not because of any medical issue

☢ It saves you having to look for a medical reason.

☢ That way, any illnesses I may have won't be picked up until they get really advanced.

Positive practises

☺ Assigning behaviours to learning disabilities or autism rather than looking for medical reasons for those changes in activity is diagnostic overshadowing, and could lead to a person's avoidable death.

☺ If necessary, do more medical checks, not fewer, so nothing is missed.

☺ Believe the families and the individual if they say a behaviour is unusual – they are the experts.

☺ If challenging behaviour is an issue and if a general anaesthetic is required, consider how many things can be done for the person at the same time e.g. taking bloods, checking teeth, MRI scan, CT scan etc.

☺ **ALWAYS consider a mental or physical health reason behind a change in the individual, including when a symptom or behaviour is new or becoming more frequent.**

Rule 7

Get frustrated at my lack of co-operation and understanding

☢ Obviously I'm being deliberately difficult to make you angry.

☢ Hospitals aren't really big, confusing, noisy places, so what's my problem?

Positive practises

☺ As mentioned in Rule 2, people with learning disabilities and those on the autism spectrum can quickly pick up on your anger and frustration and become more agitated.

☺ They are not being difficult on purpose – they're in an unfamiliar place where they don't know anyone and many may not understand why they're seeing you anyway.

☺ Talk to the family, support staff and, where possible, the individual, about the best methods of communication.

☺ Think about what the person and their carers may have had to go through just to get to the appointment. The journey itself can create stress for them so they will need a willingness from you to build a partnership to make the appointment worthwhile for everyone.

☺ Allowing more time for consultations with people with learning disabilities and those on the autism spectrum will mean that they are less likely to overrun and you will feel less time pressure.

Act like we're the first people with learning disabilities and on the autism spectrum that you've had to deal with

☢ We know that it would be easier if we didn't exist.

☢ We're someone else's problem.

☢ We don't need health care like normal people.

Positive practises

🙂 The majority of individuals with learning disabilities and those on the autism spectrum don't access the health system as they don't believe they'll get effective treatment. This needs to change.

🙂 People with learning disabilities and those on the autism spectrum need your time and attention – too many slip through the cracks. Imagine if a member of your family was being refused treatment… would you stand for it?

🙂 The more you accept that people with learning disabilities and those on the autism spectrum are entitled to treatment the more confident you will become.

🙂 See the whole person and what they say and do, leaving assumptions to one side and building rapport over time.

Rule 9

Don't try to understand what things are like for me

☢ My life is so easy, it's not like I have had to constantly adapt to try to fit in.

☢ We like being judged all the time.

Positive practises

- Take time to think about this person as an individual – See, Smile, Say Hello.

- Ask about their experience – can anything be done differently to make it better or easier?

- Think about where the person and their family and carers might be on their healthcare journey – pre-diagnosis, just diagnosed, treatment, post-treatment, recovery – and their emotional journey – anger, grief, acceptance. It all has an impact on how they may react on the day they come to see you. Your patience and understanding will have a huge impact.

- The more you can put yourself in the shoes of the person you are treating, the smoother and more effective the appointment will be.

We're just one of those difficult families, not you being difficult at all

☢ We're just attention seekers and time wasters.

☢ Don't believe a word we or our families and carers say.

Positive practises

- 😊 Trust the families and carers. Even if they can't specify exactly what's wrong, they'll know when the person with learning disabilities they are supporting is in need of medical attention and they will have noticed physical, mental and emotional changes that are causing concern.

- 😊 Just because they may not be able to articulate their needs doesn't mean they should be ignored.

- 😊 Be aware of the 'double empathy problem' (Milton, 2012). Don't dismiss a person because they can't conform to your expectations. Try changing your expectations instead.

- 😊 People with a learning disability can die avoidably because health professionals do not take the signs of ill health seriously. **ALWAYS** believe what the person or their families and support workers are saying.

- 😊 Presentation of pain can vary hugely – be open to looking for non-typical signs.

Further explanations

Rule 1: Assume that you know everything and we know nothing

Training is a vital issue in ensuring that healthcare professionals and support staff develop helpful attitudes, knowledge and skills. Many professionals who have had no training manage to get it right, but sadly many still get it wrong. Until there is training in how to build relationships with people with learning disabilities and autism from the very start of their journey through the healthcare system, they will still be at a considerable disadvantage. From a check-up with the GP to taking blood samples, to community nurses, receptionists, hospital porters, consultants or surgeons, the ability to see and interact is down to the individual professional and this can lead to a marked lack of continuity in care.

Too often, people with learning disabilities and those on the autism spectrum are denied treatment, and many have been outright *refused* treatment, because sadly the system is still set up more for the people who work within it than those who would benefit from accessing it. Even while acknowledging that there is huge demand on the resources of our healthcare system, these pressures have left no time for considering how to look after the more vulnerable members of our society. If they cannot co-operate fully with the way the system is set up then they're on their own. Which, of course, contributes to the shocking statistic of early deaths in individuals with learning disabilities, including those on the autism spectrum.

These individuals, along with carers, family members and support workers, often suggest that the most efficient way to change these statistics would be for specific training to be provided to anyone who works in the sector, right from the start of their professional lives. Ideally, people with learning disabilities and those on the autistic spectrum should be directly involved in such training in order to build communication skills and new kinds of partnerships. In the meantime, there are many different support systems being set up for health professionals and people with learning disabilities and those on the autism spectrum to ease the formation of partnerships between these two groups so that quality of care may have both more of the 'quality' and more of the 'care' that we would expect.

As you are not the expert in this area of learning disabilities (yet!), it is vital that you listen to those who are. Individuals with learning disabilities and those on the autism spectrum and their families, carers and support workers are the ones to ask initially about how best to communicate with patients if it's not immediately obvious to you. Spending a little time building a rapport with everyone involved may seem time consuming but will lead to confidence and security on both sides, which in turn will mean that follow up appointments will be faster and less stressful. Building partnerships is a crucial part of delivering health care with confidence.

Rule 2: Don't worry about how you communicate with me

A partnership will work far more efficiently and effectively than any amount of box-ticking or form-filling, and there are already a few helpful initiatives to support that. Questions have been raised as to whether these initiatives just highlight people's 'differentness' and lead to judgements being made before they have even arrived at the appointment, but sadly, until the system is truly inclusive, these will continue to be necessary.

A few examples include:

- Hospital passports – a summary of vital information about any additional needs.

- Alert systems – allowing time for reasonable adjustments to be made.

- Health folders – a crucial health record taken to every appointment for information to be logged. These can also provide a summary of health issues and additional needs.

These aids have been established through partnerships with hospitals, community teams, parents and individuals with learning disabilities and autism to create quick and easy access to essential information that will ensure efficient and results-oriented appointments. It can be very frustrating if they are not used and families have to spend time repeating information and health care histories, often incurring unnecessary distress. It is therefore worth taking a little time to look through any additional information that may be available if you can.

Furthermore, if you are armed with information about the person you are seeing and their preferred means of communication, this will reduce any discomfort you may be feeling about their 'differentness'. If you are uncomfortable with the person you are seeing, they will be able to pick up on your discomfort. Being familiar with them and their preferred means of communication will make you feel more comfortable, which in turn will put the person you are seeing at ease.

An inability to communicate should not be a factor here. There are some powerful statistics around the percentage of communication that is non-verbal, so never assume that someone who apparently lacks the cognitive ability to talk does not know what is going on. Be aware of how much you convey through the tone of your voice and your body language. Similarly, some people struggle to interpret visual clues and focus more on language, which they need to be as unambiguous as possible. While it may seem a tough ask to cover so many communication possibilities, it doesn't need to be – the more these additional ways of communicating are used and included the easier it will become.

Ask about additional methods of communication that people with learning disabilities and autism may use, be it BSL, Makaton, Books Without Words, PECS, among others.

Many community teams have learning disability nurses and can help with appointments and communication. Use their expertise and try to get them on board whenever possible.

Rule 3: Don't make allowances for my disabilities or for me being autistic

Attempting to make people fit into a system designed for others is never going to work. Each time a person fails to fit into a box gives them a sharp reminder of their differentness and magnifies their exclusion. It can only lead to people feeling lonely and isolated.

The Equality Act (2010) went some way to addressing this by insisting that *reasonable adjustments* be made for those who were not being well served by having learning disabilities. This can be as easy as just making a little more time, finding a quieter room to see families in, adjusting the lighting for anyone who has sensitivities or finding other ways to communicate – all small things that require little time and effort but can have a huge impact. And the more often it is practised the easier and more natural it will become.

While acknowledging possible acronym fatigue, the acronym TEACH illustrates these reasonable adjustments well. TEACH was developed by the Hertfordshire Learning Disability Community team and covers all the ways in which differences can be made in delivering medical knowledge and health care:

Time, **E**nvironment, **A**ttitude, **C**ommunication, **H**elp

Only by being unconventional in thinking of ways to deliver health care to those who are themselves unconventional can we start to see equality of care delivered. Think differently and act creatively.

Rule 4: Get really impatient and rush me through the appointment so you can get rid of me

Impatience and rushing appointments can be huge barriers to delivering satisfactory health care. Not only are health care professionals compromising themselves, but by doing this they are putting their patients at risk too.

Autistic people and those with learning disabilities can often need longer to process information or to formulate their responses. Furthermore, if they lack the cognitive ability to process that information then their carers, parents and loved ones are often compromised simply by the pressure of being in that situation, feeling out of their depth and bombarded by jargon and medical information.

Time and patience are needed here, along with a large dose of understanding. For the patients and their families, just getting to the appointment may have required heroic efforts, for example planning a route that is the least stressful, factoring any necessary stops for personal hygiene or tending to medical needs etc. By the time the patients and their carers reach the hospital they may need to be greeted by patient professionals who show understanding and who can adjust their attitude to manage the appointment and maximise outcomes for all. Giving autistic people and those with learning disabilities and their carers time to process information is crucial here. Invest time and energy in each interaction, not just for the moment but for the future as well. Your time will save time.

Rule 5: Look past us and only talk to our families, carers or support workers

It can be soul crushing as a parent, carer or support worker of a person with learning disabilities to watch your charge being ignored by a health professional, talking over them as if they aren't there or aren't deserving of attention, almost as though they were less than human. It is even more so for the person themselves, who is often more than aware that they are being ignored and talked over, too.

There doesn't ever seem to be any hesitation in treating babies, who can neither understand nor reply to instructions or explanations, nor can they be reasoned with. And yet, for some reason the system penalises those who grow into older children, young adults and beyond who can't tick the regular developmental boxes and co-operate with treatment and health care access. Why is this? These vulnerable adults do not deliberately avoid crossing developmental milestones and yet they are held to account for it. It is almost as if they cannot be treated unless they are a 'fully functioning adult'. Babies will be treated despite their lack of mental capacity, but not those who fail to mature into neurologically-typical adults, who do not develop the cognitive function to be able to discuss their health care needs... As if they don't face enough challenges without being denied health care as well!

Again, we come back to the necessity of building partnerships. See the whole person in front of you. How would you feel if that was your daughter, son, mother, father, brother or sister being ignored and refused health care, imagine the feelings that this would instil in you if you were sat on the other side of the room. Take a whole-person approach, don't just look at any diagnosis.

Rule 6: Assume that anything I do that you find difficult is part of my disability and not because of any medical issue

Diagnostic overshadowing can play a huge role in the early deaths of people with learning disabilities and those on the autism spectrum with learning disabilities (Blair, 2017).

Families are exhausted by the constant battle of having to convince health professionals that there really is something wrong with the people in their care. And individuals may not be able to express how they are feeling or why they are acting differently. It is too easy to use their disabilities to explain away any behaviours that may seem different.

So many assumptions are made around the expression of pain, for example. It is often assumed that pain is felt and expressed only in certain ways, and therefore if those behaviours are not observed, pain does not exist. This is both wrong and dangerous. Anyone who has expertise of caring for or supporting an individual with learning disabilities will have a story around not getting help because a person wasn't displaying the 'approved' pain indicators. Similarly, any individual who struggles with sensory issues or who is interacting with someone who is pressuring them for information, may find themselves unable to convey what they need to.

If an individual is functioning at a cognitive age level of around 18 months or less, has no language skills and no cognitive recognition of pain or how to explain it, how can we be 100% sure that if that individual starts to exhibit different behaviours it is not because of a medical issue? For parents of children and adults like this, whatever age they may grow to, it is heart breaking not knowing whether their child has stomach ache, tooth ache, head ache or sore joints etc., any of which may be a symptom of a more serious illness. These parents will do anything to ensure their child's safety and comfort and are tired of having to fight for essential health care that is so readily available to other people. Labelling is lazy and it is vital that we move on from assumptions made on the basis of a previous diagnosis.

Diagnostic overshadowing is inexcusable. If the cause of discomfort or pain isn't readily explainable then it may be a good idea do more tests rather than skip essential screening and attribute symptoms to the person's disabilities (Blair, 2017).

Rule 7: Get frustrated at my lack of co-operation and understanding

It is perfectly possible to find a way to work round any difficulties arising from a lack of co-operation or any other interference. It can seem different and possibly difficult for health professionals to do this, but be patient with your patient – again, it is worth taking a moment to try to picture the amount of stress they may be under at this time.

There is much that neurologically typical people take for granted when they access health care, but for others, the break in their routine, the sensory overload of a different journey, the anxiety of not knowing why they are going somewhere different or why they are there, and of not knowing what's expected of them, can all make them less than co-operative with no intention of being so. To them, you are one more blip in a bad day. If they knew you were there to help them they'd be suitably grateful, but they won't be able to recognise or express that they should be, so be aware of the different dynamic in these interactions.

Rule 8: Act like we're the first people with learning disabilities and on the autism spectrum that you have ever had to deal with

The huge majority of people with learning disabilities and those on the autism spectrum are never known to community teams or any health care professional. This is often because they or their carers do not think they would get the care they needed even if they did – they know all too well that any forms, literal or metaphorical, do not have boxes to tick that cover them and their needs in any way. At every turn the health care system is geared to only those who can fully understand it and co-operate with it, leaving the most vulnerable even more vulnerable. The importance of your work to change this cannot be underestimated and they must feel valued in order to seek out your expertise.

Equality of care means exactly that – everyone should have access to health care regardless of any disabilities. Your ability to enable that access, through communication, acceptance, learning and patience, will improve integration and then appointments with individuals with learning disabilities and those on the autism spectrum will be the rule rather than the exception.

While acknowledging the pressures of working within a health care system with limited resources and a huge demand on those resources, it does not necessarily require any additional resources to change the way you relate to a person with autism or learning disabilities. In fact, the more you allow yourself to treat such individuals, the more familiar you will become with what works and what doesn't. Becoming more comfortable and finding new ways to interact will itself generate confidence and improve treatment. Familiarity conquers fear and promotes inclusion. The individuals themselves can't do this, only you can. You are familiar with the way the system works – autistic people, those with learning disabilities and their families are often intimidated by their surroundings in hospitals and other healthcare settings and look to you for guidance. If you are unable to form some kind of connection then opportunities are lost. This is the time to stop looking at the people in front of you as patients, easily dismissed and with no expertise, and look at them as people who have expertise that you can learn from and need in order to do your job well.

Rule 9: Don't try to understand what things are like for me

For individuals with learning disabilities and those on the autism spectrum, and for their families, carers and support staff, nearly every aspect of their lives is a struggle; a constant battle to access the community, daily living, education, jobs, socialising and health care. Can you imagine what that is like? If you are able to imagine a life like that, just for a minute, then you will immediately realise that to have one person in the day not make life harder is a bonus. It doesn't take much; a smile, a connection, a quiet, unspoken acknowledgement that you don't mind what is happening in your room at that moment, you can work round it, with the individuals and make sure they leave the room feeling like someone has treated them with humanity and patience, not as part of some huge system which is processing them for the sake of it and anxious to spit them out the other side.

It can be difficult for individuals and their families to make the most of these appointments. Each appointment provides challenges for them and they will have good days and bad days. However, one thing they wish for more than anything is for the health professional they are seeing to acknowledge that they may be at less than their best and may need that health professional to be patient.

Yvonne's story: What I would wish for

Hospitals will always be a part of our family life – it goes with the territory when you have a child with complex needs. Even though I spend several hours, sometimes several days and nights, in hospital every month, I absolutely dread every minute we're there, and it gets harder with each passing year.

What one thing would make the whole experience more bearable? That's easy. I wish that every single hospital employee could learn how to truly listen.

Some health professionals barely listen at all. Others appear to listen, but you soon realise that it was only so they could formulate their reply. Occasionally, we meet someone very special who really listens, and with their whole selves, so they even hear what's left unsaid. They're the ones who make magic happen. As well as absorbing our words, they gain a tangible sense of what our lives are really like in a way that parents like me seldom experience.

Time stops still while compassionate kindness soothes suffering. In that moment, something profound happens; my sick child becomes the only thing that matters.

You hear and take my concerns seriously, somehow knowing this is my first adult conversation in days. You make me feel like an equal rather than someone less. You understand all I say even though I'm barely talking coherently. You help me make sense of all of my fears. You acknowledge the essence of who my broken, hurting little boy really is, barely noticing his disabilities and equipment. You make a holistic assessment based on quality of life rather than individual symptoms.

When my child doesn't co-operate with your examination, you ask for and accept my help. I suggest we turn it into a game, you play along enthusiastically.

You offer me a glimpse of the future when all health professionals are like you. When we will all pull together on the same side, working in partnership solely to enhance my child's life.

I can tell by your eyes that you know the things we haven't talked about. You recognise my exhaustion and notice how my hair hasn't seen a comb for a week, but you don't judge me or make me feel inadequate. You 'get' how my life is. A never-ending merry-go-round of sleep-deprivation, of coping with double incontinence, of tube-feeds, of nasal-cannulas, of oxygen-saturation monitors, and of the ever-present vomiting and chest physiotherapy in the middle of the night.

You know how my son's fragility terrifies me, frightened that his tenuous grip on life could slip at any moment. You feel my guilt that I can't stop his pain, and you sense how hard I work to keep him alive. You know better than to ask me how I'm coping because you know I'll always say, 'I'm fine'. You understand that that's better than me starting to cry and never being able to stop, so we don't go there. We don't have to because for that moment, you were already there, with us and for us.'

Yvonne Newbold is the author of *The Special Parent's Handbook* (2014)

(Excerpt taken from *Through Our Eyes* (Blair J et al, 2016))

Rule 10: It's just one of those difficult families, not you being difficult at all

Scepticism from health professionals is one of the worst barriers to come up against for families and carers of those with learning disabilities or autism.

Being labelled 'difficult parents' happens all the time. But what if that assumption is the wrong way round? Maybe the parents aren't the difficult ones? Maybe it's those health professionals who make assumptions about the people they see before them – people who make them uncomfortable and refuse to toe the line in a bid to get care for their children or family member in need.

'Different' does not equate to 'difficult'. Or someone may be being difficult for a good reason, which they are unable to express. Work with the people involved to find out why.

For autistic people and those on the autistic spectrum, the 'double empathy problem' clearly illustrates this issue of being unable to 'play by the rules', rules that have been set up by someone else:

'The models of autism as presented by cognitive psychological theories, much like the triad of impairments, locate the difficulties faced by autistic people solely within the brains/minds of the 'autistic person', rather than the world in which they inhabit, or in the relations and interactions people have, that can lead to a sense of total disconnection through to a mutual shared sense of "social reality". A number of sociologists view "versions of perceptual truth" as contested and negotiated in interaction. Milton (2011, 2012a) argues that the social subtext of a situation is never a given, but actively constructed in the interactions people have with one another. From this point of view, it is illogical to talk of an individual having a "social" deficit of some sort.

'Rather, that in the case of when autistic people and those not on the autism spectrum attempt to interact, it is both that have a problem in terms of empathising with each other: a "double empathy problem". Indeed, autistic writers have been talking of empathy being a 'two-way street' for many years (e.g. Sinclair, 1993). A more serious problem ensues however, when one side of an interaction are able to impose their own views of a situation onto the other. This can also lead to *the subsequent internalisation of this dominant outsider view and a loss of connection with one's sense of authentic selfhood.*

'"I had virtually no socially-shared nor consciously, intentionally expressed, personhood beyond this performance of a non-autistic 'normality' with which I had neither comprehension, connection, nor identification. This disconnected constructed facade was accepted by the world around me when my true and connected self was not. Each spoonful of its acceptance was a shovel full of dirt on the coffin in which my real self was being buried alive..." (Williams, 1996: 243).'

(Milton, 2017)

References

Blair J (2017) Diagnostic overshadowing: see beyond the diagnosis. *British Journal of Family Medicine* Jan/Feb 17 pp34–35.

Blair J, Busk M, Goleniowska H, Hawtrey-Woore S, Morris S, Newbold Y & Nimmo S (2016) Through our eyes: What parents want for their children from health professionals. In: S Hardy, E Chaplin & P Woodward (2016) *Supporting the Physical Health Needs of People with Learning Disabilities: A handbook for professionals, support staff and families*. Hove: Pavilion Publishing & Media.

Blair J (2013) Everybody's life has worth: getting it right in hospital for people with an intellectual disability and reducing clinical risks. *Clinical Risk* **19** (3) 58–63.

Heslop P, Blair P, Fleming P, Hoghton M, Marriott A & Russ L (2013) *Confidential Inquiry into Premature Deaths of People with Learning Disabilities (CIPOLD)* [online]. Bristol: Norah Fry Research Centre 2013. Available at: http://www.bristol.ac.uk/media-library/sites/cipold/migrated/documents/fullfinalreport.pdf (accessed September 2017).

Hollins S & Hollins M (2005) *You and Your Child: Making sense of learning disabilities*. London: Karnac Books.

Newbold Y (2014) *The Special Parents Handbook*. Poole: Amity Books by CMP (UK).

Milton D (2017) *A Mismatch of Salience: Explorations of the nature of autism from theory to practice*. Brighton and Hove: Pavilion Publishing & Media.

Useful websites and resources

British Institute of Learning Disabilities (BILD)
www.bild.org.uk
BILD helps develop the organisations that provide services and the people who give support.

Books beyond Words
www.booksbeyondwords.co.uk
Publishes accessible stories in pictures to help people with learning and communication disabilities explore and understand their own experiences.

CHANGE
www.changepeople.org
A human rights organisation led by disabled people.

Disability Matters

www.disabilitymatters.org.uk
An e-learning resource to enhance understanding and skills of staff.

Down's Side Up

www.downsideup.com
Gently changing perceptions of Down's Syndrome.

Easyhealth

www.easyhealth.org.uk
Provides over 250 free accessible leaflets, health guides and videos.

Mencap

www.bacdis.org.uk/policy/documents/
Gettingitright.pdf
A group of organisations working towards better healthcare, well-being and quality of life for people with a learning disability.

NHS Choices, Going into Hospital with a Learning Disability

www.nhs.uk/Livewell/
Childrenwithalearningdisability/Pages/Going-into-hospital-withlearning-disability.aspx
Information on preparing a person with a learning disability for hospital.

Syndromes Without a Name SWAN UK
www.undiagnosed.org.uk/

University of Hertfordshire
www.intellectualdisability.info/
Understanding learning disability and health

Yvonne Newbold
yvonnenewbold.com
Doing whatever it takes to make life easier for special needs families and the staff who work with them.

Useful training and development resources from Pavilion Publishing

Pavilion Publishing (www.pavpub.com) publishes a range of resources for staff working in learning disability and autism. Here are some of the range of products available.

Successful Health Screening through Desensitisation for People with Learning Disabilities: A training and resource pack for healthcare professionals

By Lisa Harrington and Sarah Walker

Supporting the Physical Health Needs of People with Learning Disabilities: A handbook for professionals, support staff and families
Edited by Steve Hardy, Eddie Chaplin and Peter Woodward

Taking Control of My Health: A training manual for health and social care staff to deliver a course for people with learning disabilities who have health conditions
By Mary Codling

Supporting Women with Learning Disabilities through the Menopause: A manual and training resource for health and social care workers
By Michelle McCarthy and Lorraine Millard

Understanding Emotions in People with Learning Disabilities: Factsheets to help staff understand and manage emotions of sadness, anxiety and anger in people with learning disabilities
By Surrey and Borders Partnership NHS Foundation Trust

A Mismatch of Salience: Explorations of the nature of autism from theory to practice

The collected writings of Dr Damian Milton.

Ten Rules for Ensuring Autistic People and People with Learning Disabilities Develop Challenging Behaviour... and maybe what to do about it

By Dr. Damian Milton and Richard Mills with Simon Jones

Autism and Intellectual Disability in Adults, Volumes 1 and 2

Edited by Dr Damian Milton and Professor Nicola Martin

Understanding and Supporting Children and Adults on the Autism Spectrum: A training and learning resource

By Julie Beadle-Brown and Richard Mills